THE BRIDGE TO RACIAL UNITY

WITH TASHA MORRISON, STEPHANIE NANNEN, AND JUDY WU DOMINICK

Be The Bridge To Racial Unity
Published by Orange, a division of The reThink Group, Inc.
5870 Charlotte Lane, Suite 300
Cumming, GA 30040 U.S.A.

The Orange logo is a registered trademark of The reThink Group, Inc.

ISBN: 978-1-63570-064-0

©2017 Be the Bridge

Authors: Latasha Morrison, Stephanie Nannen, Judy Wu Dominick
Graphic Design: Jacob Hunt
Project Manager: Nate Brandt

Scripture quotations are taken from the Holy Bible, New Living Translation, copyright © 1996, 2004, 2007, 2013, 2015 by Tyndale House Foundation. Used by permission of Tyndale House Publishers, Inc., Carol Stream, Illinois 60188. All rights reserved.

First print edition published by Orange Books.

For additional resources like this, visit www.BetheBridge.com and www.OrangeBooks.com.

Printed in the United States of America
First Edition 2017

1 2 3 4 5 6 7 8 9 10

09/29/17

CONTENTS

PROLOGUE

On the night before Jesus was crucified He prayed this prayer for His church:

> Jesus looked up to heaven and said, "Father, the hour has come. Glorify your Son so he can give glory back to you. For you have given him authority over everyone. He gives eternal life to each one you have given him. And this is the way to have eternal life—to know you, the only true God, and Jesus Christ, the one you sent to earth. I brought glory to you here on earth by completing the work you gave me to do. Now, Father, bring me into the glory we shared before the world began.
>
> "I have revealed you to the ones you gave me from this world. They were always yours. You gave them to me, and they have kept your word. Now they know that everything I have is a gift from you, for I have passed on to them the message you gave me. They accepted it and know that I came from you, and they believe you sent me.
>
> "My prayer is not for the world, but for those you have given me, because they belong to you. All who are mine belong to you, and you have given them to me, so they bring me glory. Now I

am departing from the world; they are staying in this world, but I am coming to you. Holy Father, you have given me your name; now protect them by the power of your name so that they will be united just as we are. During my time here, I protected them by the power of the name you gave me. I guarded them so that not one was lost, except the one headed for destruction, as the Scriptures foretold.

"Now I am coming to you. I told them many things while I was with them in this world so they would be filled with my joy. I have given them your word. And the world hates them because they do not belong to the world, just as I do not belong to the world. I'm not asking you to take them out of the world, but to keep them safe from the evil one. They do not belong to this world any more than I do. Make them holy by your truth; teach them your word, which is truth. Just as you sent me into the world, I am sending them into the world. And I give myself as a holy sacrifice for them so they can be made holy by your truth.

"I am praying not only for these disciples but also for all who will ever believe in me through their message. I pray that they will all be one, just as you and I are one—as you are in me, Father, and I am in you. And may they be in us so that the world will believe you sent me.

"I have given them the glory you gave me, so they may be one as we are one. I am in them and you are in me. May they experience such perfect unity that the world will know that you sent me and that you love them as much as you love me. Father, I want these whom you have given me to be with me where I am. Then they can see all the glory you gave me because you loved me even before the world began!

"O righteous Father, the world doesn't know you, but I do; and these disciples know you sent me. I have revealed you to them, will continue to do so. Then your love for me will be in them, and I will be in them." (John 17)

Jesus, we wrote this discussion guide with the hope that You would use it to help Your church become a better answer to Your prayer.

INTRODUCTION

"I am in them and you are in me. May they experience such perfect unity that the world will know that you sent me and that you love them as much as you love me."

—John 17:23

The journey toward racial unity is not an easy process.

It can feel daunting to dive into the unknown abyss of racial conversations. It takes courage to move toward what is uncomfortable and unnatural. Many of us look around and see racial divides. Things feel stuck, and we want to do something. We have read the Scriptures and prayed for unity. But how do we, the body of Christ, actually become one? How can the words in John 17 come alive in each of us and in our communities? How does unity begin to permeate our entire being? How do we become light in a dark world full of racial division? How do we become a witness and a voice for racial unity?

The purpose of this discussion guide is to help us get unstuck. It is designed to facilitate conversations that have the potential to heal racial divides—a first step in our collective journey toward racial reconciliation. This guide will aid you as you navigate conversations and work to build relationships. Our ultimate goal is to achieve racial reconciliation as a reflection of our ministry of reconciliation in Christ. The concept of racial unity—many differently shaped, differently functioning body parts coming together to form a single, unified body of Christ—provides a foundational framework for the work we must do to achieve this goal.

How is this Guide to be used?

This guide is designed to be used in a racially diverse, small group setting. The content of the guide relies on individual members to share their experiences and work through the reconciliation process with one another. A leader's guide is available (and highly recommended) to help prepare for and facilitate each of the nine sessions. Each session focuses on a different topic and is guided by Scripture, prayer, discussion, and relevant background information.

What are the goals of this Guide?

- For God to be glorified

- For the church to be credible

- For Christians to develop biblical tools that empower them to be the bridge between people divided by racial and cultural differences, and thereby bring healing and transformation to communities

Who is this Guide for?

- Are you heartbroken by the racial divide in your country, your city, your church, or your family?

- Do you want to experience greater diversity, richness, and depth in your relationships?

- Do you want the church to demonstrate God's heart for all people groups to the world?

- Do you feel fearful and awkward about connecting with others of a different race?

- Can you no longer tolerate the injustice, apathy, and fear you see around you?

- Would like the church to be a distinct and transformative voice in the conversation on racial healing?

If you answered yes to any of these questions, then this study is for you. It is designed to provide tools and support for individuals and groups interested in the process of gospel-based racial bridge building.

What can I expect from engaging in this process?

One of the most daunting aspects of embarking on a journey like this is not knowing what to expect. It may be helpful to think of it as you would any aspect of your Christian discipleship—a Spirit-led rearrangement of categories, assumptions, values, and beliefs.

- You'll develop greater awareness of God's desire for people of every tongue, tribe, and nation to form a unified body in Christ.

- You'll be given tangible steps to take in order to transform your current views and vision regarding racial diversity.

- You'll have your assumptions and stereotypes challenged and your world-view expanded.

- You'll begin to bring interracial healing and transformation into your sphere of influence.

What will be required of me?

- Humility and openness to learning new things
- Listening to—and really hearing—others
- Willingness to trust God and take risks
- Commitment to the process, even when it gets difficult
- Disconnecting from privilege and power

Welcome to the work of racial reconciliation.

As you embark on this journey, know that you are following in the footsteps of other bridge builders who have pursued and found reconciliation with their brothers and sisters in Christ from all races and backgrounds. May God help you find a group willing and excited to step into these broken places in the body of Christ, to watch what He will do.

THE BRIDGE TO TRUTH

Belief in the existence of absolute truth is foundational to the Christian faith, as is belief in a loving God who knows and reveals truth. "Righteousness and justice are the foundation of your throne. Unfailing love and truth walk before you as standards" (Psalm 89:14). Jesus makes it plain that He is the truth of God embodied: "I am the way and the truth and the life. No one comes to the Father except through me" (John 14:6).

And yet when it comes to historical truth, we're often satisfied with partial truth. Elie Wiesel, survivor of the Holocaust, explained why in his Nobel Prize lecture:

> *Of course we could try to forget the past. Why not? Is it not natural for a human being to repress what causes him pain, what causes him shame? Like the body, memory protects its wounds. When day breaks after a sleepless night, one's ghosts must withdraw; the dead are ordered back to their graves.*

He went on, however, to issue a call to remember both good and evil:

> *But for the first time in history, we could not bury our dead. We bear their graves within ourselves. For us, forgetting was never*

an option. Remembering is a noble and necessary act. The call of memory, the call to memory, reaches us from the very dawn of history. No commandment figures so frequently, so insistently, in the Bible. It is incumbent upon us to remember the good we have received, and the evil we have suffered.[1]

Note how God called the Israelites to remember their period of slavery in Egypt:

> "The Lord your God will soon bring you into the land he swore to give you when he made a vow to your ancestors Abraham, Isaac, and Jacob. It is a land with large, prosperous cities that you did not build. The houses will be richly stocked with goods you did not produce. You will draw water from cisterns you did not dig, and you will eat from vineyards and olive trees you did not plant. When you have eaten your fill in this land, be careful not to forget the Lord, who rescued you from slavery in the land of Egypt." (Deuteronomy 6:9–12)

And He called them pass down knowledge of their history to their children as they taught them God's laws:

> "In the future your children will ask you, 'What is the meaning of these laws, decrees, and regulations that the Lord our God has commanded us to obey?' Then you must tell them, 'We were Pharaoh's slaves in Egypt, but the Lord brought us out of Egypt with his strong hand. The Lord did miraculous signs and wonders before our eyes, dealing terrifying blows against Egypt and Pharaoh and all his people. He brought us out of Egypt so he could give us this land he had sworn to give our ancestors. And the Lord our God commanded us to obey all these decrees and to fear him so he can continue to bless us and preserve our lives, as he has done to this day." (Deuteronomy 6:20–24)

What does a comprehensive narrative of American history look like? Unlike that of Israel, the historical narrative of the United States is not of one people group but many. And American history can look quite different depending on whose memories we excavate: Native Americans, African Americans, Latino Americans, Asian Americans, or Anglo-European Americans. Our greatest challenge is finding a way to weave all the segregated memories into a single tapestry. Navajo writer Mark Charles refers to this challenge as an endeavor to create a *common memory*. In the book *Lies My Teacher Told Me: Everything Your American History Textbook Got Wrong*, James Loewen explains, "American History is important. More than any other topic, it is about us. Whether one deems our present society wondrous or awful or both, history reveals how we arrived at this point. Understanding our past is central to our ability to understand ourselves and the world around us."[2]

In our first three sessions, we will look at the steps we must take on the **BRIDGE TO TRUTH** in order to move toward true racial reconciliation. The first step is **AWARENESS**. As mentioned already, awareness for many of us requires a significant expansion of our knowledge of history.

Once we become aware of truth, we must fully acknowledge it. **ACKNOWLEDGMENT** is a powerful way to see our own brokenness, as well as the brokenness we have inherited. As we acknowledge the part we've played in creating and sustaining racial disunity, we can then begin to envision our role in forging racial solidarity.

When God begins to open our eyes to the racial injustice around us—things that are unsatisfactory, unreasonable, or unfair—we begin to recognize our own complicity, or participation, in it. This new sense of awareness can provoke uncomfortable feelings of **SHAME AND GUILT**. If we are to process these emotions well, we need tools to help us navigate their dynamics within both our souls and our communities. We will discuss a biblical framework for shame and guilt that will help us appreciate their redemptive potential.

SESSION 1
AWARENESS

2 CORINTHIANS 5:14–21

Either way, Christ's love controls us. Since we believe that Christ died for all, we also believe that we have all died to our old life. He died for everyone so that those who receive his new life will no longer live for themselves. Instead, they will live for Christ, who died and was raised for them.

So we have stopped evaluating others from a human point of view. At one time we thought of Christ merely from a human point of view. How differently we know him now! This means that anyone who belongs to Christ has become a new person. The old life is gone; a new life has begun!

And all of this is a gift from God, who brought us back to himself through Christ. And God has given us this task of reconciling people to him. For God was in Christ, reconciling the world to himself, no longer counting people's sins against them. And he gave us this wonderful message of reconciliation. So we are Christ's ambassadors; God is making his appeal through us. We speak for Christ when we plead, "Come back to God!" For God made Christ, who never sinned, to be the offering for our sin, so that we could be made right with God through Christ.

Background

A group of forty-seven Christian leaders from six continents—and some of the most conflict-ridden countries in the world—joined forces to create a theological vision for reconciliation as God's mission in a world filled with destructive conflicts. They came to define reconciliation as "God's initiative, restoring a broken world to His intentions by reconciling 'to himself all things' through Christ: the relationship between people and God, between people themselves, and with God's created earth. Christians participate with God by being transformed into ambassadors of reconciliation."[3]

The first step in the biblical reconciliation process is **AWARENESS**. The *Oxford English Dictionary* defines awareness as "knowledge or perception of a situation or fact."

Because so much of our country remains racially segregated along geographic lines, it's possible for people to live for many years without any awareness that relationships between racial groups are still broken and in need of reconciliation.[4] Perhaps you were taught to be "colorblind"—to "look beyond" someone's race and see them simply as a human being. While there are often good intentions behind this colorblind approach, it actually nurtures a problematic type of blindness, or unawareness, about our country's racial history and its current racial realities. For this reason, it ends up doing more unintended harm than accomplishing intended good.

Awareness begins with listening to and hearing others.

Discussion Questions

1. What experience in your life has been most influential in making you the person you are today?

2. Tell a story about a time when someone of another culture made an assumption about your culture and it caused you harm. How did that make you feel?

3. Describe your ethnic culture. What is one thing you love about your own culture and one thing you wish were different?

4. What difference would it make if diversity were more of a reality in our friendships? In our schools and communities? In the church?

5. What is the difference between *diversity* and *racial reconciliation*?

6. If we are all created in the image of God (the imago Dei), what does that say about ethnic diversity? What does that say about the nature of God?

7. What are some ways we can celebrate our differences?

Prayer

All-knowing God, help us, Your bride the Church, to become more aware! God, give us a willingness to study our past for the purpose of seeing how it has affected our present, and how it will affect our future. Give us the grace to use this understanding to help further the kingdom of God here on earth as it is in heaven. In Jesus' name, amen.

NICOLE KING

Homework

- If you are doing this study in a group context with a leader's guide, at the end of your group time, you should have received a note card with the name of someone from the group. Write a note to the person whose name is on the card you receive.

- Visit a church congregation of a different ethnicity, or create an experience that involves racial diversity (for instance, shop in an ethnically distinct part of town, attend a concert where you'll hear music of another culture, try a restaurant featuring another culture's food).

Supporting Scriptures

Colossians 1:19–22

James 2:8–9

Additional Reading

Debby Irving, *Waking Up White: And Finding Myself in the Story of Race* (Elephant Room Press, 2014).

James W. Loewen, *Lies My Teacher Told Me: Everything Your American History Textbook Got Wrong* (The New Press, 2007).

SESSION 2
ACKNOWLEDGMENT
AND LAMENT

JAMES 4:8–10

Come close to God, and God will come close to you. Wash your hands, you sinners; purify your hearts, for your loyalty is divided between God and the world. Let there be tears for what you have done. Let there be sorrow and deep grief. Let there be sadness instead of laughter, and gloom instead of joy. Humble yourselves before the Lord, and he will lift you up in honor.

Background

After we become aware of brokenness, loss, and injustice, the second step on the bridge to truth is **ACKNOWLEDGMENT**. For believers, acknowledgment of brokenness, injustice, and loss produces **LAMENT**.

To lament is to express grief, sorrow, or regret over something unsatisfactory, unreasonable, or unfair. We may lament about wrongs done to us, wrongs done to others by others, or wrongs we ourselves have committed. We may lament about losses we have experienced, losses others have experienced, or losses we have inflicted. In lament, we acknowledge both our own brokenness and the brokenness of the world.

We must acknowledge the historical causes of the racial divides in our country and the reality that we have inherited the consequences of a long history of racial injustices. These consequences include educational, justice, and economic systems still tainted by racial disparities. **We must also acknowledge the part we have played in this injustice, whether wittingly or unwittingly, so we may envision our role in the solutions.**

Discussion Questions

1. What have you learned since our last time together? How has God worked in your life to raise your awareness of the need for racial reconciliation in our country?

2. Tell us a story about racism—either something involving you personally or something you observed.

3. Define *lament*. Why is lament an important step in the work toward racial unity?

4. How have your family dynamics affected your perspective on race? What biases (whether explicit or implicit) do members of your family hold toward people of different racial and ethnic groups? Do you find it difficult to address issues of racism in your family? What do you lament about your family in the area of racial justice?

5. How can you personally reflect a greater acknowledgment of the truth of our country's racial history?

Prayer

Father, may we have the strength and courage to acknowledge the truth of our country's past. As we move forward, may we acknowledge that there are systems and laws in place that are not for all people. May we have the courage to stand up and seek out these truths. May we love our neighbors as we love ourselves. May we have the courage to ensure that those sitting at our table fully reflect Your kingdom. Amen.

JEN WICKSTROM

Homework

- Before the next session, share a meal with the person you were paired with.

- Write out some of the things you've learned about race relations in America since this group began. Have any of the things you've read or heard led you to lament? Take some time to write out your lament, then read your lament out loud. Be prepared to share with and listen to others during your next group time.

- Create a genogram. A genogram is a family diagram that can be thought of as an elaboration on the family tree. Genograms provide a way of mapping relational dynamics and identifying family patterns across several generations. Diagram your family's race dynamics using the genogram. This visual can assist in identifying where you may have derived your racial perspectives and stereotypes.

Supporting Scriptures

Lamentations

Romans 12:9–15

Additional Reading

Soong Chan-Rah, *Prophetic Lament: A Call for Justice in Troubled Times* (IVP Books, 2015).

Bryan Stevenson, *Just Mercy: A Story of Justice and Redemption* (Spiegel & Grau, 2015).

Isabel Wilkerson, *The Warmth of Other Suns: The Epic Story of America's Great Migration* (Vintage Books, 2011).

Your Genogram

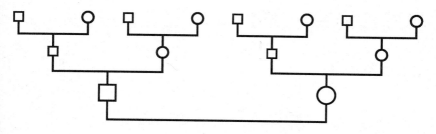

RELATIONSHIP	RELATIONAL DYNAMICS	SYMBOL
RACISM	Hatred or intolerance of—or presumed superiority toward—another race or other races.	□〰〰〰○
CUT OFF	People in the family stop talking to one another or avoid contact due to interratial marriage or adoption.	□—‖—○
PREJUDICES	Preconceived opinion that is not based on reason or actual experience within relationships.	□-----○
ENMESHMENT	Pressure is created for family members to think, feel, and act alike. There is low tolerance for people to be separate, to disagree or to be different.	□═══○
ABUSE	A severe crossing of personal boundaries—whether they be verbal, emotional, or physical—severely injuring the dignity and humanity of another.	□▨▨▨▨○

SESSION 3
SHAME AND GUILT

EZRA 9:5–6

I stood up from where I had sat in mourning with my clothes torn. I fell to my knees and lifted my hands to the Lord my God. I prayed, "O my God, I am utterly ashamed; I blush to lift up my face to you. For our sins are piled higher than our heads, and our guilt has reached to the heavens."

Background

The steps of **AWARENESS** (Session 1) and **ACKNOWLEDGMENT AND LAMENT** (Session 2) of racism and racial injustice can generate uncomfortable feelings of **SHAME AND GUILT.** In our individualistic and therapeutic culture, shame and guilt tend to be regarded with suspicion—or as tools for controlling others. Viewed this way, they can hinder the process of relational restoration. In the Bible, however, shame and guilt are much more.

The Scriptures do contain examples of people who endured humiliation at the hands of others (Noah, Joseph, a delegation of King David's men).[5] But two other important sources of shame include (1) when guilt and wrongdoing are exposed,[6] and (2) sharing an identity with a group that has sinned and/ or acted dishonorably,[7] so that even if a person has not personally sinned, she or he loses status and communal esteem *(communal shame).*[8]

Shame and guilt related to the latter two actually have redemptive potential. They can restore alienated individuals and communities to both God and one another. But our ability to appreciate redemption like this may require a closer look at how culture shapes our perceptions of and responses to shame and guilt.

Western morality is based on *individual guilt and innocence* (for instance, a person who obeys the law is "good," but one who breaks the law is "bad" and deserves to be punished). It reflects the assumption that the individual is the primary unit and source of identity, accountability, and status. For this reason, people from individualistic cultures struggle to grasp the concept of collective shame, or a morality based on *communal honor* (or, where individuals share responsibility in the preservation of a community's integrity and reputation). Communal honor exists somewhat in American culture. If your toddler pushes a kid at the park, for example, you apologize on his or her behalf. If a father makes a scene at a high-school football game in front of his daughter and her peers, she feels embarrassed. In general, however, when communal shame is aroused beyond the level of familial association, which frequently happens in conversations about racial inequality, it is rapidly countered with proclamations of individual innocence—"*I* didn't do anything wrong! *I'm* not a racist!" The following story illustrates cultural differences in the way people handle collective shame and guilt.

In January 2017, Sam Okyere, a Ghanaian television personality living in South Korea, shared his experiences of racism in the country on the Korean talk show *As You Say*. One of the cohosts responded, "I'm embarrassed." The cohost next to him said, "I feel so sorry." The third chimed in, "I am sorry." The immediate response of the three Korean cohosts was empathy and apology rather than condemnation of the specific people who had mistreated Sam. Their responses reflected an ethic based on communal honor: as a country, South Korea had failed to exercise appropriate hospitality to Sam, and Koreans collectively bore that dishonor. Given a similar situation, *Americans* would not likely feel dishonored as Americans due to their perceptions of individual guilt or innocence (thinking, "*Those people were guilty of racism, but their behavior doesn't reflect poorly on me*").

Ancient Hebrew culture as recorded in the Bible contains themes of communal shame and honor that are similar to those in Korean culture. In several places, we see Israel's righteous leaders sharing the collective shame and even guilt of the people. Ezra, personally innocent of the sins committed by the people, prays, "O my God, *I* am utterly ashamed; *I* blush to lift up my face to you. For *our* sins are piled higher than *our* heads, and *our* guilt has reached to the heavens" (Ezra 9:6, emphasis added). Daniel likewise confesses, "O Lord, *we* and *our* kings, princes, *and ancestors* [even deceased ancestors!] are covered with shame because *we* have sinned against you" (Daniel 9:8, emphasis added).

Although communal shame brings great distress here, it's part of a redemptive arc. For both Ezra and Daniel, shame is not associated with fear of punishment or the need to establish personal innocence; it is about recognizing the opportunity to initiate communal restoration. As members of a group, they assume the responsibility of confessing and seeking reconciliation on behalf of the entire group. **The possibility of communal restoration through communal identity and repentance increases the ways we can achieve justice and restore peace between estranged ethnic groups.**

Prejudice and discrimination against people of other tongues, tribes, and nations are sins as old as humanity, and they require the same process of transformation as any other sin. Let's examine our hearts together.

Discussion Questions

1. Were you raised in a more communal or more individualistic culture? With a guilt/innocence–based morality or an honor/ shame–based morality? How do you think these factors affect the way you process feelings of shame and guilt? Which conversations about race and racism trigger feelings of guilt and shame in you? How do you typically respond?

2. Can you think of an occasion in which feelings of shame and guilt led to negative outcomes for yourself or your relationships?

3. Can you think of an occasion in which feelings of shame and guilt over wrongdoing led you to repentance?

4. How does the gospel—the work of Jesus Christ in His death, burial, and resurrection—address our shame and guilt?

Prayer

Father, I have experienced the shame of being different, unwelcomed, and "less than" as a person of color. At the same time, I acknowledge the guilt and shame that I have carried both for myself and as a member of Your church for how we have failed in pursuing reconciliation through our acts of commission or omission. This mix of shame and guilt both as one who has been a recipient and perpetrator of prejudice and racism has incapacitated me at times. I need Your healing to cleanse me from my shame and guilt. Please make me into the reconciler You intend me to be in the world. Amen.

KAREN YANG

Homework

- Discuss with a friend any personal shifts in your heart or other discoveries you've made through this study so far.

- If you have children, purchase for them a book, doll, or other toy that represents an ethnicity different from yours.

Supporting Scriptures

Psalm 34:4–5

Psalm 51

Proverbs 14:9

Isaiah 1:16–18

Daniel 9:1–19

Additional Reading

Roland Muller, *Honor and Shame: Unlocking the Door* (Xlibris, 2001).

Jayson Georges and Mark D. Baker, *Ministering in Honor-Shame Cultures: Biblical Foundations and Practical Essentials* (IVP Academic, 2016).

THE BRIDGE TO JUSTICE

The Acholi people in Northern Uganda have a traditional justice process called *Mato Oput*. Its goal is to achieve reconciliation between clans affected by either an intentional murder or accidental killing. Key elements of the process include accountability, forgiveness, compensation or reparations, and restoration of both the wounded community and the offending party. It is a model of *restorative justice*, which contrasts sharply with the *retributive* and *punitive justice* meted out by most modern Western criminal court systems.

The first step in *Mato Oput* is truth telling, which takes on the form of negotiations. Witnesses from both sides are invited to share what they know until all parties can reach a consensus on what took place. In complicated cases, this initial step can take years. It's not rushed, because the possibility of reconciliation itself hinges on the alienated parties' ability to establish a common understanding of events.

We have experienced in our last several sessions together that truth telling in the context of racial bridge-building can resemble negotiations as members of different racial groups share what they know with each other, and learn what they do not know from each other. During this process, lack of awareness can burgeon into awareness, and painful silence or denial can give way to healing acknowledgment. But, as we discussed in our last session, truth telling that implicates racialized sin in us also tends to provoke feelings of guilt and shame.

When accompanied by a fear of condemnation, feelings of guilt and shame can lead to deflection, defensiveness, distancing, victim blaming, and abandonment of the conversation. Or, at the other extreme, guilt and shame can produce a driven activism that hasn't been adequately seasoned by thoughtful self-examination. In contrast, when harnessed by the liberating truth of the gospel, which offers radical forgiveness through undeserved mercy and grace, these same emotions can lead to **CONFESSION** and **REPENTANCE**—actions that set the stage for both personal and communal transformation.

When feelings and interactions become painful and tense, it's helpful to keep in mind that the end goal of truth telling about racism and racialized sin is not condemnation and punishment, but healing for both victims and perpetrators of racial sin and violence. Perpetrators experience conviction of sin by the Holy Spirit, acknowledge their guilt, and receive forgiveness and restoration. Victims receive acknowledgment and validation of their pain, suffering, and loss. And all experience the healing and liberation that forgiveness enables. All are restored. These are the fundamental elements of restorative justice.

Gregory Boyle is a Jesuit priest who, for over two decades, has worked closely with gang-involved youth and their communities in Los Angeles. He has witnessed up close the grievous cycle of senseless violence, unjust loss, grief, and retaliation—and the unforgiveness that perpetuates it. He has also witnessed the transformative power of compassion and forgiveness for both victims and victimizers:

> Isn't the highest honing of compassion that which is hospitable to victim and victimizer both? . . . [Jesus] doesn't suggest that we cease to love those who love us when he nudges us to love our enemies; nor does Jesus think the harder thing is the better thing. He knows it's just the harder thing. But to love the enemy and to find some spaciousness for the victimizer as well as the victim resembles more the expansive compassion of God. That's why you do it. To be in the world who God is.[9]

SESSION 4
CONFESSION

JAMES 5:16

Confess your sins to each other and pray for each other so that you may be healed. The earnest prayer of a righteous person has great power and produces wonderful results.

PROVERBS 28:13

People who conceal their sins will not prosper, but if they confess and turn away from them, they will receive mercy.

Background

In the reconciliation process, once people become aware of either sins they've actively committed against another party or sins in which they've neglected to do what is just and good, their next step is **CONFESSION.**

Confession can be difficult because of the humility it requires. It means agreeing with God about the sinfulness of our actions and naming our specific offenses (such as, "I lied about this particular thing" rather than a generic, "I'm not perfect.")

Confession also feels risky because it involves vulnerability, and fear of vulnerability may tempt us to avoid confessing our sins. But it's important to consider that there's also tremendous risk in *not* confessing our sins. Keeping our sins hidden from others (even though nothing can be hidden from God) by withholding confession to those we've harmed short-circuits the reconciliation process and traps us in our guilt and shame. It prevents us from experiencing forgiveness, growth, and peace.

In any relationship, whether with God or people, taking responsibility for our sins is essential to creating and maintaining real intimacy. **Unacknowledged sin hurts relationships.**

May the Spirit lead us along the pathway of confession. May we find freedom from dark thoughts and feelings that need the transformation of the cross.

Discussion Questions

1. How has the Lord transformed your heart since Session 1?

2. Divide into groups of two or three. Discuss two things you want to see the Lord do in your heart concerning your thoughts on race. Why is confession important to the work of reconciliation?

3. What have you learned about healthy racial relationships from the group?

4. What do you find most difficult about confessing your sins related to race?

5. Reread Proverbs 28:13 at the beginning of this chapter and discuss. Are you in the habit of regularly confessing your sin? How does confession affect your relationship with God? With others?

Prayer

Lord, I am grateful for Your desire and provision for me to be free—free from beliefs that deceive and oppress me, my family, and my neighbors and prohibit us from reflecting the fullness of Your glory. In, by, and through You, I am pulling down false beliefs that oppose Your character and truth. Help me do whatever it takes to change and walk in a renewed identity—a reflection of Your glorious image. In the name of Jesus, amen.

LUCRETIA BERRY

Homework

Spend time alone with God in confession. Agree with Him about any sin that comes to mind. Make sure to confess any biases you may carry against other races. Examine whether any of these things was passed down to you through your family of origin. Then sit quietly before God and ask Him to reveal any hidden sin in your life.

Begin learning about the racial history of your town. Visit any nearby museums or exhibits featuring the civil rights movement of the 1960s or other racial history.

Supporting Scriptures

Psalm 32

1 John 1:9

Additional Reading

Walter Brueggemann, *Prayers For A Privileged People* (Abingdon Press, 2008).

Richard Twiss, *Rescuing the Gospel from the Cowboys: A Native American Expression of the Jesus Way* (IVP Books, 2015).

SESSION 5
FORGIVENESS

LUKE 17:3–4

"So watch yourselves! If another believer sins, rebuke that person; then if there is repentance, forgive. Even if that person wrongs you seven times a day and each time turns again and asks forgiveness, you must forgive."

EPHESIANS 4:31–32

Get rid of all bitterness, rage, anger, harsh words, and slander, as well as all types of evil behavior. Instead, be kind to each other, tenderhearted, forgiving one another, just as God through Christ has forgiven you.

Background

Whether someone has hurt you or you have done harm to another person, **FORGIVENESS** is for you. It is difficult to forgive those who have sinned against us, and extending grace to those who have hurt us can be a hard task. Finding a way to forgive those who continually hurt us probably feels impossible. Yet one person changing his or her attitude and feelings can make all the difference in the world.

Forgiveness is a divine act. To forgive doesn't mean we've chosen to simply ignore or gloss over the evil and injustice we've experienced or committed. It also doesn't mean that we deny or spiritualize away feelings of anger or grief, which are normal emotions of a wounded heart. It does mean, however, that we choose to release the offender from the debt he or she owes us, to give up our "right" to retaliate. Jesus modeled divine forgiveness for us when He took upon himself all the evil, sin, and injustice of the world (including those of every person reading this), then willingly suffered and absorbed the wrath we deserved.

We are all guilty and in need of forgiveness (Romans 3:23). And we have been forgiven on account of Christ. C. S. Lewis wrote, "To be a Christian means to forgive the inexcusable because God has forgiven the inexcusable in you."[10] In other words, we forgive because we ourselves have been forgiven (Matthew 18:21–35). Forgiving others is the most Christlike act there is. It is costly and painful, yet transformative and life giving. Of course, the process of becoming like Christ in this way does not happen overnight. We must receive grace from God and extend it to others as we all struggle together to be transformed. As Martin Luther King, Jr. said, "Forgiveness is not an occasional act; it is a permanent attitude."[11]

Discussion Questions

1. Why is forgiveness an act you do for you more than for the person or circumstance you are forgiving?

2. Confession of sin by perpetrators and forgiveness of sin by those who have been sinned against are both indispensable in the process of racial reconciliation. Discuss what you think would happen if either of these were lacking.

3. How do you forgive when those you are trying to forgive continuously hurt you? What does it mean to have a "permanent attitude" of forgiveness in this situation, rather than the "occasional act"?

4. How do you forgive yourself? What do you personally need to be forgiven for?

5. What characteristics in your life might indicate that you haven't fully forgiven past hurts, even if you know in your head what you need to do?

Prayer

Jesus, we come with humble hearts; we are in need of Your forgiveness. We ask that You would heal the wounded places of our hearts. Help us remain committed to the work of reconciliation, choosing to love our neighbors as we love ourselves. May we be quick to forgive those who have hurt us. May Your love and grace bring peace to our weary souls. Amen.

FAITH BROOKS

Homework

- Pray and write out your grievances: those things you need to forgive and those things you need to be forgiven for. Ask the Lord to instruct you.

- Pray for someone you still need to forgive. (If you need help with what to pray for, use the prayers in the Bible. Some good examples include John 17, Ephesians 1:17–21, Ephesians 3:16–20, Philippians 1:3-6, 9–11, Colossians 1:3–14, 1 Thessalonians 5:23–24.) After you pray, write that person a note as an exercise, even if you're not yet ready to give it to him or her.

Supporting Scriptures

Psalm 103:12

Micah 7:18–19

Additional Reading

Martin Luther King, Jr., *Strength To Love* (1963).

Desmond Tutu and Mpho Tutu, *The Book of Forgiving: The Fourfold Path for Healing Ourselves and Our World* (HarperOne, 2014).

SESSION 6
REPENTANCE

ACTS 3:19

Now repent of your sins and turn to God, so that your sins may be wiped away.

2 CORINTHIANS 7:10

The kind of sorrow God wants us to experience leads us away from sin and results in salvation. There's no regret for that kind of sorrow. But worldly sorrow, which lacks repentance, results in spiritual death.

Background

Confession of previous or current wrongdoing is a vital step in the reconciliation process, but it's not enough just to admit what we have done in the past or are still doing in the present. If we desire reconciliation, we must also change our future behavior and direction. This change is called **REPENTANCE.**

Repentance involves turning away from sin and toward God. It means discontinuing our sinful behavior, renouncing our allegiance to idols, and throwing ourselves fully into God's merciful arms.

Repentance requires that we adopt a whole new point of view on the matter or circumstance before us. **As we surrender our old ways of thinking and step out onto a new path, God can do His work of transformation.**

A. W. Tozer said,

> *"Let us beware of vain and overhasty repentance, and particularly let us beware of no repentance at all. We are a sinful race . . . and until the knowledge has hit hard, until it has wounded us . . . it has done us no good. A man can believe in total depravity and never have any sense of it for himself at all. Lots of us believe in total*

depravity who have never been wounded with the knowledge that we've sinned. Repentance is a wound I pray we may all feel."[12]

Discussion Questions

1. What is your greatest hindrance or barrier to personal transformation?

2. Why are we sometimes blind to our own sins but fully aware of the sins of others?

3. What do you think Tozer means by repentance being a "wound"?

4. What ideologies do you need to let go of in order to move forward in the process of racial reconciliation?

5. Why is true repentance so difficult? What do we as a country need to repent of in the area of racial injustice?

6. How can we ensure that these conversations we've been having about race and racial division don't end with this study, but continue and become a regular part of our lives?

Prayer

Father, forgive us for our silence and for turning a blind eye to the pain of our brothers and sisters. We repent of the times we've seen anyone as anything less than beautiful, unique, and created in Your image. Give us new hearts to appreciate the value of every person and the courage to be voices for dignity and justice. In Jesus' name, amen.

HEATHER OLDHAM

Homework

- Identify one thing in the area of racial sin where you believe God is calling you to repent. Take a concrete step toward repenting, whether it involves confessing something out loud to a friend, initiating an uncomfortable conversation, releasing judgment or contempt, diversifying your social circle, expanding your reading options, choosing to sit under the teaching of someone you have subconsciously excluded as a teacher until this point, or something else.

- Create something—a simple drawing, a poem, an essay, a painting, a mosaic, a sculpture, a song, or whatever else comes to mind—that reflects how God is working in your heart through this study. Share it with someone.

Supporting Scriptures

Lamentations 3:40

Ezekiel 14:6

Mark 1:15

James 4:8–10

Additional Reading

Mae Elise Cannon, Lisa Sharon Harper, Troy Jackson, and Soong-Chan Rah, *Forgive Us: Confessions of a Compromised Faith* (Zondervan, 2014).

Ibram X. Kendi, *Stamped from the Beginning: The Definitive History of Racist Ideas in America* (Nation Books: 2016).

THE BRIDGE TO RECONCILIATION

"Reconciliation is an ongoing spiritual process involving forgiveness, repentance, and justice that restores broken relationships and systems to reflect God's original intention for all creation to flourish."

—Brenda Salter McNeil

By now, you have figured out one of the reasons our country remains segregated: *racial reconciliation is hard work.* Entering into honest conversations and building deep friendships with people outside of our natural affinity groups require commitment, humility, empathy, and sacrifice. It's costly, demanding, and often emotionally exhausting.

That's because true biblical reconciliation involves much more than superficial, feel-good conversations that end in hugs and handshakes. The New Testament Greek word that gets translated into the English word "reconciliation" is *katallasso*. It was a term originally used by money changers, meaning "to change, or exchange, as coins for others of equivalent value."[13] When people are at odds with one another, one of the defining characteristics of their enmity is their common inability or refusal to see things from each other's perspective. To a great extent, estranged parties' ability to "change places" and exchange perspectives with each other becomes a critical component of biblical reconciliation. If we pay attention, we see that themes of changing places or *walking in each other's shoes* as a bridge to reconciliation exist even in literature and popular entertainment, such as Mark Twain's *The Prince and the Pauper*, the movies *Freaky Friday*, *Trading Places*, *Soul Man*, and others.

Changing places with our enemies is ultimately a Christlike act. When we were still God's enemies, God made Christ, who had never sinned, to be sin *for us*, so that we could be made right with God (Romans 5:8–10; 2 Corinthians 5:21). Jesus modeled for us the reality that changing places with our enemies involves taking up a cross, denying the self, and laying down your life. By the world's standards, it's inadvisable, if not absurd. Yet without death—without crucifixion—there can be no new life, no resurrection. Jesus explained: "I tell you the truth, unless a kernel of wheat is planted in the soil and dies, it remains alone. But its death will produce many new kernels—a plentiful harvest of new lives" (John 12:24).

Maybe that sounds like more than you bargained for, but it's important that we realize the gravity of what we're asking of each other and ourselves. When God called us to the work of brokering reconciliation and unity among His estranged children, He was asking us to become bridges where enemies could begin the process of *Christlike exchange*.

When alienation exists at the level of societal groupings, it almost always involves a history of one group having abused power over another—of people having given in to the very temptations with which Satan baited Jesus in the wilderness: to abuse practical everyday power, to abuse religious power, and to abuse political power (Luke 4:1–13).[14] Throughout human history, when nations and people groups have given into these temptations, they have committed large-scale injustices against other nations and people groups: wars of conquest, captivity, forced labor and exploitation, genocide, creation and maintenance of social hierarchies and caste systems, breaking treaties and covenants, and wrongful imprisonment. These injustices warp the image of God in both victims and oppressors.

That's why biblical reconciliation has such a strong restorative justice component to it. Author Andy Crouch says, "Justice is restoring authority to the vulnerable and vulnerability to the powerful."[15]

No matter where you are in this process, we encourage you to press on. The Scriptures remind us, "So let's not get tired of doing what is good. At just the right time we will reap a harvest of blessing if we don't give up" (Galatians 6:9). And, "Be strong and immovable. Always work enthusiastically for the Lord, for you know that nothing you do for the Lord is ever useless" (1 Corinthians 15:58). We need to stay in the game, stay in the Word, and stay on our knees. The story of the gospel reveals the nature of our God, who forms light from darkness, hope from despair, friendship from hatred, beauty from ashes, and victory from defeat.

SESSION 7
REPARATION

PHILEMON 1:1, 3–21

This letter is from Paul, a prisoner for preaching the Good News about Christ Jesus . . .

I am writing to Philemon, our beloved co-worker . . .

May God our Father and the Lord Jesus Christ give you grace and peace.

I always thank my God when I pray for you, Philemon, because I keep hearing about your faith in the Lord Jesus and your love for all of God's people. And I am praying that you will put into action the generosity that comes from your faith as you understand and experience all the good things we have in Christ. Your love has given me much joy and comfort, my brother, for your kindness has often refreshed the hearts of God's people.

That is why I am boldly asking a favor of you. I could demand it in the name of Christ because it is the right thing for you to do. But because of our love, I prefer simply to ask you. Consider this as a request from me—Paul, an old man and now also a prisoner for the sake of Christ Jesus.

I appeal to you to show kindness to my child, Onesimus. I became his father in the faith while here in prison. Onesimus hasn't been of much use to you in the past, but now he is very useful to both of us. I am sending him back to you, and with him comes my own heart.

I wanted to keep him here with me while I am in these chains for preaching the Good News, and he would have helped me on your behalf. But I didn't want to do anything without your consent. I wanted you to help because you were willing, not because you were forced. It seems Onesimus ran away for a little while so that you could have him back forever. He is no longer like a slave to you. He is more than a slave, for he is a beloved brother, especially to me. Now he will mean much more to you, both as a man and as a brother in the Lord.

So if you consider me your partner, welcome him as you would welcome me. If he has wronged you in any way or owes you anything, charge it to me. I, Paul, write this with my own hand: I will repay it. And I won't mention that you owe me your very soul!

Yes, my brother, please do me this favor for the Lord's sake. Give me this encouragement in Christ. I am confident as I write this letter that you will do what I ask and even more!

Background

With every successive session, we have explored an additional layer of requirements for true reconciliation between estranged groups to take place. So far, we have covered awareness, acknowledgment and lament, shame and guilt, confession, forgiveness, and repentance. The next step is for wrongdoers to work together with those they have wronged in order to **make things right.** Since unjust events can sometimes feel historically distant, another way to say this is that those who have inherited the power and benefits of past wrongdoers must work together with those who have inherited the burdens and vulnerabilities of those who were victimized. This process is called **REPARATION**. Merriam-Webster defines reparation as "the act of making amends, offering expiation, or giving satisfaction for a wrong or injury." It is the work of repairing the relationships between individuals and communities that have been broken by injustice, including racism.

While *reparation* is a term we don't often hear outside of activist circles, it is a thoroughly biblical concept. We find specific instructions about reparation woven throughout the Mosaic civil laws, and stories about restitution sprinkled throughout the Scriptures. Almost always, restitution involves not only repayment of an amount owed, but also payment of an additional fee or percentage. Take Numbers 5:7, for example, where God tells Moses what people must do when they do wrong to another person: "They must confess their sin and make *full restitution for what they have done*, adding an additional 20 percent and returning it to the person who was wronged" (emphasis added). The Hebrew root word for *reparation* in God's instruction to Moses is *shuwb*, and it is used close to one thousand times throughout the Old Testament.

Perhaps the best-known New Testament example of reparation is the story of Zacchaeus, the tax collector. In that day, tax collectors regularly abused their power to extort additional tax payments from the people. They then pocketed the excess. But when Zacchaeus came face-to-face with Jesus, he declared, "I will give half my wealth to the poor, Lord, and if I have cheated people on their taxes, I will give them back four times as much!" (Luke 19:8).

Note how concrete reparations are. They consist of actions that improve people's circumstances. In the face of injustice, there can be no reconciliation without such action. Curtiss DeYoung explains, "Systems of injustice in society and in the church exact a heavy cost on those outside the centers of power and effectively block reconciliation" and "declaring that we are equal without repairing the wrongs of the past is cheap reconciliation."[16]

Let's consider an example to which we can all relate. Say I own a gift shop. Business is so good that I hire an additional employee to assist me. My new employee, Scott, and I agree that I will pay him five hundred dollars week. Scott and I work alongside each other for several weeks, and everything appears to be going well. But one day, Scott pulls me aside and says, "Hey, you agreed to pay me five hundred dollars a week, but you've only been paying me three hundred dollars a week."

I feel horrible because the discrepancy was caused by a clerical oversight. I want to make things right, so I acknowledge my mistake and ask for Scott's forgiveness, which he grants. I promise that I will always pay him the correct amount from now on. Have I made things right? Are we reconciled?

No, not until I pay him the missing two hundred dollars a week for his past weeks' work. I need to make reparations. It also wouldn't hurt for me to throw in a fifty-dollar gift card to be spent in the shop for his troubles. God certainly made such an allowance for those who suffered wrong in Numbers 5:7.

Sometimes reparation involves money, as in the example above. This type of *reparation* is called *restitution*. Do you remember the Greek word often translated into the English as "reconciliation," *katallasso*?

This same word was also used to convey the concept of "settling up" (or reconciling) financial accounts. Reparation might also take the form of creating previously unavailable opportunities or closing advantage gaps for those who have suffered marginalization.

In our practice of restorative justice, reparation is not punitive in nature. Reparation is not about paying a fine for a wrong committed or assuaging a guilty conscience. Instead, reparation acknowledges that through historical injustice, some communities lost (or had stolen from them) opportunities, possessions, property, wealth, and safety, so that other communities could obtain more of those things than what they were due. **Reparation is about repaying what is owed and working toward equity for all.**

Discussion Questions

1. What reconciliation principles can you glean from Paul's work in repairing the relationship between Onesimus and Philemon? What risks did Paul take in initiating the reparation? What were the potential risks for Onesimus? For Philemon? What was the reparation going to cost Paul, Onesimus, and Philemon?

2. How is the desire to make reparations (like Zacchaeus expressed) different from guilt? How is reparation related to the concepts of *equality* and *equity*?

3. What could reparations look like in the context of the racial dynamics of America?

4. For racial reconciliation to happen in the American church, what are some of the costs the majority culture will need to pay? What price will communities of color have to pay?

Prayer

Lord, make us ambassadors of reconciliation. Teach us to speak Your words of truth and forgiveness. Transform our hearts so we may bring wholeness to the broken hearts and systems in our country. Use us to tear down the barriers that continue to divide Your body. Show us the ways we can participate in healing wounds and restoring justice. Give us boldness to bridge divides and willingness to pay the cost. In Your holy and redemptive name, amen.

ELIZABETH BEHRENS

Homework

- Tell others about your journey so far through this reconciliation process. Consider writing down your story and sharing it with others.

Supporting Scriptures

Numbers 5:5–7

2 Samuel 9:1–13

Additional Reading

Allan Boesak and Curtiss Paul DeYoung, *Radical Reconciliation: Beyond Political Pietism and Christian Quietism* (Orbis, 2012).

SESSION 8
RESTORATION

JOHN 21:9–17

When they got there, they found breakfast waiting for them— fish cooking over a charcoal fire, and some bread.

"Bring some of the fish you've just caught," Jesus said. So Simon Peter went aboard and dragged the net to the shore. There were 153 large fish, and yet the net hadn't torn.

"Now come and have some breakfast!" Jesus said. None of the disciples dared to ask him, "Who are you?" They knew it was the Lord. Then Jesus served them the bread and the fish. This was the third time Jesus had appeared to his disciples since he had been raised from the dead.

After breakfast Jesus asked Simon Peter, "Simon son of John, do you love me more than these?[a]"

"Yes, Lord," Peter replied, "you know I love you."

"Then feed my lambs," Jesus told him.

Jesus repeated the question: "Simon son of John, do you love me?"

"Yes, Lord," Peter said, "you know I love you."

"Then take care of my sheep," Jesus said.

A third time he asked him, "Simon son of John, do you love me?"

Peter was hurt that Jesus asked the question a third time. He said, "Lord, you know everything. You know that I love you."

Jesus said, "Then feed my sheep."

Background

The ultimate aim of reconciliation is the **RESTORATION** of broken relationships, whether between individuals or entire communities. As you have learned, true reconciliation requires commitment and sacrifice from both sides. Sometimes the two sides move through the reconciliation process at different speeds. Not everyone is ready for restored relationships or the cost of restoring them.

The entire reconciliation process up to this point has focused on correcting the past. **Through restoration, we begin to build a future together.** Restoration occurs when people and communities work to heal each other, support each other, provide safety for each other, share resources, learn from each other, break bread in each other's homes, labor alongside one another toward common goals, build a common language, and laugh together.

One nation that has committed to do the hard work of reconciliation is the country of Rwanda. For decades, the Hutu and Tutsi ethnic groups despised each other. This culminated in the Rwandan genocide of 1994. Over a period of one hundred days, the Hutu majority slaughtered approximately eight hundred thousand Tutsi minorities. An additional two million Rwandans were displaced. Yet now, over twenty years later, hundreds of stories of reconciled relationships between Hutus and Tutsis have been written because, as a nation, Rwanda committed itself to an official truth and reconciliation process. It hasn't been perfect, by a long shot; but it has been beautiful, restorative, and hope-filled.

Discussion Questions

1. In the passage from John 21 above, we see a picture of Jesus working to restore his relationship with Peter, who had previously denied and abandoned him (John 18). What observations can you make about the way they interacted with each other?

2. What factors, if any, do you recognize as obstacles to racial reconciliation in your church? Your community? Our nation?

3. Think back through all the sessions we've had (awareness, acknowledgment and lament, guilt and shame, confession, forgiveness, repentance, reparation). In which stage do you think people tend to get stuck, so that true restoration is hindered?

4. How do you address prejudiced comments from friends or family? How have they responded to you bringing this subject to light in the past? Has anything you've learned from this study influenced how you might approach situations like these in the future?

5. When you are in the middle of conflict with others and emotions start to run high, do you tend to move toward or away from the other person? Why do you think you respond that way?

6. How can we continue work toward restoration in this small group? How can we work toward restoration in our broader community?

7. Think about your spheres of influence: home, workplace, children's schools, place of worship, and the like. What would it look like for you to start pursuing restoration in those spaces?

Prayer

God, breathe Your whole being back into this place. Fill it with Your majesty and glory. Drop us to our knees at how much bigger You are in this state. Restore us to life-giving people, not life-taking ones. Remind us whose we are before we tell someone else who they should be in our anger and frustration. Forgive us when we ask You to show up the way we want. Remind us that the ones we think need changing are actually here to change us. In Jesus' name, amen.

ROBYN AFRIK

Homework

Conduct your own research on the reconciliation process Rwanda entered into following the 1994 genocide, as well as other similar efforts in other nations like South Africa and Canada. Write down your responses to these stories, and reflect on what principles you can take from their efforts and apply to your own life, and to our nation.

Spend time in prayer, asking God what He is calling you to next in the area of racial reconciliation. How can you take the next step to share what you have learned with others? Be prepared to discuss this topic in your next group time.

Supporting Scriptures

Matthew 5:23–25

Ephesians 2:16–22

Colossians 1:19–22

Additional Reading

Christena Cleveland, *Disunity in Christ: Uncovering the Hidden Forces that Keep Us Apart* (IVP Books, 2013).

Brenda Salter McNeil, *Roadmap to Reconciliation: Moving Communities into Unity, Wholeness and Justice* (IVP Books, 2016).

SESSION 9
REPRODUCTION

2 CORINTHIANS 5:14–21

Either way, Christ's love controls us. Since we believe that Christ died for all, we also believe that we have all died to our old life. He died for everyone so that those who receive his new life will no longer live for themselves. Instead, they will live for Christ, who died and was raised for them.

So we have stopped evaluating others from a human point of view. At one time we thought of Christ merely from a human point of view. How differently we know him now! This means that anyone who belongs to Christ has become a new person. The old life is gone; a new life has begun!

And all of this is a gift from God, who brought us back to himself through Christ. And God has given us this task of reconciling people to him. For God was in Christ, reconciling the world to himself, no longer counting people's sins against them. And he gave us this wonderful message of reconciliation. So we are Christ's ambassadors; God is making his appeal through us. We speak for Christ when we plead, "Come back to God!" For God made Christ, who never sinned, to be the offering for our sin, so that we could be made right with God through Christ.

Background

Our study has now come full circle. We have walked through awareness, acknowledgment and lament, guilt and shame, confession, forgiveness, repentance, reparation, and restoration. Now we will finish with same passage of Scripture we started with.

In our first session, we discussed how the church and its people are to be credible witnesses for the unity we find in Christ. As Christ's ambassadors, we are called to the work of reconciliation, the work of making things right. This means actively sharing the gospel message with others, helping to restore all people to a right relationship with God. But it also includes working to reconcile people to each other and to the rest of God's creation.

One beautiful outcome of reconciliation is that it creates space to draw others in. The Trinity displays the perfect example of this. The Father, Son, and Holy Spirit continuously relate to each other in perfect love, unity, mutuality, and yet diversity. The joy they experience through their intimacy propels them to chase after and welcome others into their relationship. As each of us are pulled into this relationship and experience its amazing dynamic, we are compelled to share about it with those around us, hoping to persuade them to join us. We don't merely enjoy the fruit of reconciliation ourselves, but through **REPRODUCTION** we continually widen our circle to include more people, creating an ever-expanding community of shalom.

Each of us has a different part to play in this work. Each of us brings a different set of gifts, experiences, strengths, and passions. We are to bring our whole selves, ready to live and work alongside others in all our diversity, in order to display an unlikely unity, all for God's glory.

Discussion Questions

1. As you read through 2 Corinthians 5 above, what stood out to you? Reconciliation takes place on whose initiative?

2. How does our being reconciled to Christ relate to our being reconciled to each other?

3. What does it mean to be Christ's ambassadors?

4. How is the ministry of reconciliation that Paul writes about in 2 Corinthians relevant to the healing of racial divisions in our country?

5. What are some of the particular strengths, passions, and experiences God has gifted you with? How do you see God using those in the work of reconciliation?

6. How is God leading you to become more engaged with the process of racial reconciliation? What are your next steps?

Prayer

Lord, make us ambassadors of reconciliation. Give us Your eyes of awareness; open our ears that we may hear You. Allow us to see others as You see them. Teach us to speak Your words of truth and forgiveness. Continue to transform our hearts so we may bring wholeness to those who are broken. Lord, use us to tear down the barriers that continue to divide Your body. Help us to become beacons that will penetrate the darkness of the world we live in. We ask that You would make us one. We ask that the oneness of Your church become a credible witness for Your Glory, in Jesus' name. Amen.

LATASHA MORRISON

Supporting Scriptures

Matthew 5:14–16

Luke 12:48

Hebrews 12:13–15

Additional Reading

See following page

ADDITIONAL RESOURCES
FOR CONTINUED LEARNING AND GROWTH

James H. Cone, *The Cross and the Lynching Tree* (Orbis Books, 2011).

Robin DiAngelo, *What Does It Mean to Be White?: Developing White Racial Literacy* (Peter Lang, 2012).

Michael O. Emerson and Christian Smith, *Divided by Faith: Evangelical Religion and the Problem of Race in America* (Oxford University Press, 2001).

Drew G.I. Hart, *Trouble I've Seen: Changing the Way the Church Views Racism* (Herald Press, 2016).

David P. Leong, *Race and Place: How Urban Geography Shapes the Journey to Reconciliation* (IVP Books, 2017).

Bryan Loritts, *Letters to a Birmingham Jail: A Response to the Words and Dreams of Dr. Martin Luther King* (Moody Publishers, 2014).

Soong-Chan Rah, *Many Colors: Cultural Intelligence for a Changing Church* (Moody Publishers, 2010).

Soong-Chan Rah, *The Next Evangelicalism: Freeing the Church from Western Cultural Captivity* (InterVarsity Press, 2009),

Sandra Maria Van Opstal, *The Next Worship: Glorifying God in a Diverse World* (InterVarsity Press, 2016).

NOTES

1 Elie Wiesel, "Hope, Despair and Memory" (Nobel Lecture, Oslo City Hall, Norway, December 11, 1986), Nobelprize.org, http://www.nobelprize.org/nobel_prizes/peace/laureates/1986/wiesel-lecture.html

2 James Loewen, Lies My Teacher Told Me: Everything Your American History Textbook Got Wrong
(New York: The New Press, 2007), 2.

3 Paper Task Force, World Vision International Peacebuilding and Reconciliation Department. "Reconciliation as the Mission of God: Christian Witness in a World of Destructive Conflicts," January, 2005, https://divinity.duke.edu/sites/divinity.duke.edu/files/documents/cfr/reconciliaton-as-the-mission-of-god.pdf.

4 Dustin Cable, "The Racial Dot Map," Weldon Cooper Center for Public Service, Demographics Research Group, University of Virginia, July 2013, http://demographics.coopercenter.org/Racial-Dot-Map/.

5 Genesis 9:22; Genesis 37:12–36; 2 Samuel 10:1–5.

6 Genesis 2:25; 3:7; 2 Chronicles 30:15.

7 Ezra 9:5–15; Daniel 9:1–19.

8 Job 10:15; Proverbs 3:35; Jeremiah 46:12.

9 Greg Boyle, Tattoos On the Heart: The Power of Boundless Compassion (New York, NY: Free Press,
2010), 67.

10 C. S. Lewis, The Weight of Glory (1949; repr. New York: Harper Collins, 2001), 183.

11 Martin Luther King, Jr., Strength to Love (1963; repr. Minneapolis: Fortress Press, 2010), 33.

12 A. W. Tozer, "Three Faithful Wounds" in Man: The Dwelling Place of God: What It Means to Have Christ Living in You, compiled by Anita M. Bailey (Camp Hill, PA: Wing Spread Publishers, 2008).

13 Thayer and Smith, The NAS New Testament Greek Lexicon, s.v. "Katallasso," http://www.biblestudytools.com/lexicons/greek/nas/katallasso.html.

14 This particular explanation of Jesus' temptations comes from Richard Rohr, "First Sunday of Lent: Temptations Are Attractions to Partial Goods," in Wondrous Encounters: Scripture for Lent (Cincinnati, OH: Franciscan Media, 2011).

15 Andy Crouch, Twitter post, October 5, 2016, 10:11 a.m., https://twitter.com/ahc/status/783716218087800832.

16 Curtiss DeYoung. Coming Together: The Bible's Message in an Age of Diversity (Valley Forge, PA: Judson Press, 1995), 13, 106.

ABOUT

In 2012 Latasha Morrison felt discontent. As she drove through the heart of Austin, Texas, she asked God, "Why am I here? Why did you lead me so far from my family and my community on the East Coast?" God replied, *I brought you here to be a bridge.*

So Tasha gathered a diverse group of friends to talk about what this might mean, and together they began to form a vision. They said, "We believe that if people could come together as equals, at a table like this, with open Bibles and humble, prayerful hearts, to talk to each other honestly and, more importantly, really listen to each other, we could change the story of race in our country."

Tasha's friends committed to meeting together regularly. They would open up the Scriptures, talk, listen, laugh, cry, and pray. Between meetings, they educated themselves about our country's racial history. Sure enough, over time, each person's life was changed. And they all agreed that if every person in our country had the opportunity to take part in a group like theirs, real healing along racial lines could take place.

That's how Be the Bridge was born. The sessions in this discussion guide are based on the questions Tasha's first group investigated. Thousands of lives have been changed since then, all because of this simple idea.

Be the Bridge became an official 501(c)(3) nonprofit organization in 2016 and has expanded to include more tools, training groups and workshops, and consulting services. Our mission is to inspire the church to have a distinctive and transformative response to racial division; to equip bridge builders to develop vision, skills, and hearts for racial unity; and to partner with existing organizations who have a heart for diversity, racial justice, restoration, and reconciliation.

For information about how to get more involved with the BTB movement, check out our website at www.bethebridge.com.